Journal M.A.G.I.C. – A five-step process to create your magic is a daily journal workbook designed to assist everyone from care-givers, healthcare practitioners, life coaches and self-help industries, to individuals looking for a valuable tool. This guided journal was initially designed as a daily, self-care tool exclusively for my clients. It is comprised of five chapters: **Meditations, Affirmations, Gratitude, Intentions and Connections** and is intended to track and enhance a person's healing journey.

Each chapter contains a suggested exercise that flows into each subsequent chapter. Your journal entries are like pebbles cast into a still pond, and your written thoughts, ideas and insights are the waves that create the concentric circles rippling out from the locus point. You are the connection to the pebble, the water, and each ripple. You create a wave of change through your action, ripple after ripple, consciously and unconsciously.

Our thoughts and actions expand into effects that flow outward, creating endless possibilities in the course of our lives – ripple after ripple, chapter after chapter.

Each chapter creates momentum into the next chapter, thus creating a tidal wave of creativity, insight and effect more far reaching than you can imagine.

Enjoy your Journal M.A.G.I.C. Journey.

Journal
M.A.G.I.C.

A five step process to create your magic.

Meditation

Affirmations

Gratitude

Intentions

Connections

Created By Martez Schembri, RMT;CST-D: CFS

BALBOA.
PRESS
A DIVISION OF HAY HOUSE

Testimonials

"I have often said "Everyone has a story, so what. It's what you do with that story that counts." Truly Martez has taken a horrific accident that could have kept her in bondage and not only found her way to a deeper understanding for herself, but has created this wonderful journal for you. This is a practical step-by-step book to help you go from being stuck in your story to living a life of abundance and gratitude."

Daniel Gutierrez, Author, Speaker,
World Transformational Leader and Radio Personality
www.danielgutierrez.com

"Martez Schembri has created a powerful tool in her Journal M.A.G.I.C. workbook. If you want to enhance your healing journey, this book will help you take control and create a tidal wave of wellness in your life!"

Denise Marek, author of CALM: A Proven Four-Step
Process Designed Specifically for Women Who Worry
www.denisemarek.com

"Journal Magic is a powerful and simple tool to implement deep change. Martez Schembri's personal journey into the rebuilding of her body and life provides great insight to the innate sacredness of all life's occurrences. When life presents us with a detour from our current way of being, Martez shows us how we are actually being provided with a new and magical pathway IN, to a greater & brighter life!"

Gina SKY Tomé, Sound Shaman, Vibrational Alchemist, Teacher and Founder of The Gaia Sky™ Learning Centre www.GaiaSky.com

"An incredible outline of the fundamental ingredients for a magnificent life!"

Jairek Robbins, Results Strategist, Speaker www.jairekrobbins.com

"Journal M.A.G.I.C. provides a clear and simple pathway for those seeking true transformation in their journey towards inner healing and personal wellness. As you seek to explore your life's challenging concerns, this workbook helps you to understand the importance of persistence and focus, and offers techniques to achieve spiritual equilibrium – the genuine reflection of a healthy you. Let this book be the instrument that leads you to that breakthrough."

Beth McBlain, Author, Editor Principle of Maverick Business Consulting

Journal
M.A.G.I.C.

A five step process to create your magic.

Meditation

Affirmations

Gratitude

Intentions

Connections

Created By Martez Schembri, RMT;CST-D: CFS

BALBOA
PRESS
A DIVISION OF HAY HOUSE

Journal M.A.G.I.C.
Copyright © 2012 Martez Schembri

Editor-in-Chief: Beth McBlain
Editor: Lily-Ann MacDonald, CPM, DPA
Design: Eddie Chan

ISBN: 978-1-4525-5794-6 (sc)
ISBN: 978-1-4525-5795-3 (e)
ISBN: 978-1-4525-5796-0 (hc)

Library of Congress Control Number: 2012916657

Balboa Press books may be ordered through booksellers or by contacting:

Balboa Press
A Division of Hay House
1663 Liberty Drive
Bloomington, IN 47403
www.balboapress.com
1-(877) 407-4847

Because of the dynamic nature of the Internet, any web addresses or
links contained in this book may have changed since publication and
may no longer be valid. The views expressed in this work are solely those
of the author and do not necessarily reflect the views of the publisher,
and the publisher hereby disclaims any responsibility for them.

The author of this book does not dispense medical advice or prescribe the use
of any technique as a form of treatment for physical, emotional, or medical
problems without the advice of a physician, either directly or indirectly. The
intent of the author is only to offer information of a general nature to help you
in your quest for emotional and spiritual well-being. In the event you use any
of the information in this book for yourself, which is your constitutional right,
the author and the publisher assume no responsibility for your actions.

Balboa Press rev. date: 10/22/2012

Contents

Please cut out the tabs and place them in each of the following sections by the right edge of the page where the heading is:

Meditation: p. 13

Affirmations: p. 55

Gratitude: p. 95

Intentions: p. 135

Connections: p. 175

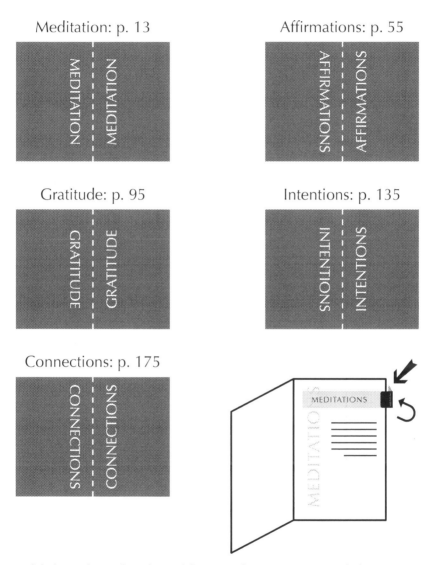

Fold the tab at the dotted line and wrap it around the paper edge of the heading. **_Please note:_** The tabs are not self-adhesive. They require you to use an adhesive agent of your choice. We recommend using double-sided tape.

*The Universe favors the brave.
When you resolve to
lift your life
to its highest level,
the strength of your soul
will guide you
to a magical place
with magnificent treasures.*

Robin Sharma
Author, Motivational Speaker

Foreword

Journal M.A.G.I.C. was born out of many years of learning, feeling and observing what tools are needed to heal spirit, body and mind. Starting with Meditation, then making Affirmations of your evolving wellness, you then become Grateful for what you have and you develop the Intention of being better. The Connections component is when you pull all these tools together to realize that we have the curative powers within us to heal ourselves by integrating spirituality, physicality and emotionality.

The Journal M.A.G.I.C. workbook is a tool that evolved as the result of my own long recovery and journey toward finding balanced spiritual, physical and emotional health. I would like to share my story with you.

Setting the Intention for this Journal M.A.G.I.C. Workbook

My intention for Journal M.A.G.I.C. is to assist you by providing the techniques that will help you extract the greatest value and experience possible from your work throughout this book.

May we all learn to flow with our life's purpose, through deepening our discovery and creation of magic in our life. Begin the ripple effect in growth, service and transformation of ourselves, others, our community, the world and the universe. It is my profound honor to have this opportunity to share this journey with you.

"Thy will be done" … and so it is.

Introduction

Journal M.A.G.I.C. – A Five Step Process to Create Your Magic is a daily journal workbook designed to assist anyone who is called to use it: from care-givers, healthcare practitioners, life coaches and self-help industries, to individuals looking for a valuable tool. This guided journal was initially designed as a daily, self-care tool exclusively for my clients. It is comprised of five chapters: Meditations, Affirmations, Gratitude, Intentions and Connections and is intended to track and enhance a person's healing journey.

Each chapter contains a suggested exercise that flows into each subsequent chapter. Your journal entries are like a pebble cast into a still pond, and your written thoughts, ideas and insights are the waves that create the concentric circles rippling out from the locus point. You are the connection to the pebble, the water, and each ripple. You create a wave of change through your action, ripple after ripple, consciously and unconsciously.

Our thoughts and actions expand into effects that flow outward, creating endless possibilities in the course of our lives – ripple after ripple, chapter after chapter.

Each chapter creates momentum into the next chapter, thus creating a tidal wave of creativity, insight and effect more far reaching than you can imagine.

Enjoy your Journal M.A.G.I.C. journey.

My Story

My story begins in 1987, when I was vacationing in Florida and was involved in a motor vehicle accident … a head-on collision. My injuries were devastating, leaving the right side of my body badly broken – including my ankle, femur, knee joint, breastbone, ribs, and two vertebrae. As if that wasn't enough, the crash severed two tendons in my right hand, caused multiple soft tissue injuries that included whiplash, and left me with numerous lacerations from an explosion of glass. It was a horrendous moment that changed my life in an instant.

Up until that time, I had been a very active, independent 24 year-old working as a clothing designer. Suddenly I found myself in a hospital, beginning the first of seven surgeries that would occupy my next four years, and marking the beginning of many more years of therapy. In addition to exhausting physical therapy, I also needed extensive psychotherapy to help me cope with the sudden and traumatic changes to my body, my mind and my life.

I was left unable to work for several months, and began the arduous routine of daily appointments with doctors, specialists, therapists, and physical rehabilitation clinics. This became my full time job, attending appointments and trying to rehabilitate myself. I knew very little about the human body, and I put my trust in the hands of the healthcare professionals. I was in a lot of pain and in a full leg cast and arm cast, which allowed me very little mobility. Initially, I needed a wheelchair to get around, but eventually this progressed to forearm crutches, because the severed tendons in my right hand made regular crutches impossible. I needed help with everything from combing my hair, to dressing and putting on my shoes. I had to sleep in the living room for months, because I couldn't manage the stairs up to my bedroom.

My Own Journey Begins…

I couldn't even imagine the years of various therapies, therapists, doctors and specialists that lay ahead of me. I would occasionally experience intense pain that I knew felt different from the pain I had become used to. When I expressed this to my health professionals, they dismissed it as being caused by my extensive bruising and swelling. Even though it didn't seem right to me, with no medical training, how could I challenge them on this point?

It wasn't until much later that we discovered several injuries had been misdiagnosed, and some were overlooked altogether. As a result, I became increasingly aware of everything around me, very guarded and hyper-vigilant. I would jump at the slightest noise or movement close to me, thinking I would get hurt again. In my paranoia, I developed a very affected awareness and hyper-sensitivity. I soon realized I had to learn to listen to my body in a new way, and when I did, my body would guide me and stop me if I didn't listen.

I began researching and reading self-help, health, psychology, self-growth and personal development books. One specific book, "Heal Your Body" by Louise L. Hay, stated that *"It awakens within you the ability to contribute to your own healing process. For us to become whole and healthy, we must balance body, mind and spirit. We need to take good care of our bodies. We need to have a positive mental attitude about ourselves and about life. And we need a strong spiritual connection. When these three things are balanced, we rejoice in living."*

I began to observe things from this new perspective, and learned about this new spirit, body, mind reality, and awareness of which I was previously not conscious. With this new interest in my body, what it had to say, and why it reacted as it did, I began implementing tools and techniques that allowed me to take a more active role in my rehabilitation, self-care and personal growth. I was already beginning my new magical journey into healing the spirit, body and mind.

My New Calling...

I suddenly became convinced of my new calling. I decided to leave the security of my job and educate myself by going back to school to become a Registered Massage Therapist and Craniosacral Therapist. I knew I wanted to help people because I could genuinely empathize, support, encourage and inspire them on their journey to healing their own spirit, body and mind.

During my massage therapy training, while studying the signs and symptoms of Post Traumatic Stress Disorder (PTSD), I found myself identifying with each symptom. This was a bitter sweet realization – another misdiagnosis – and yet, a relief because it captured how I had been struggling for so long.

I began 'talk therapy' for prolonged periods of time, working with many different disciplines, but I was not experiencing results as quickly as I had hoped. My body was still over-reacting and hyper-vigilant. I knew there was something being overlooked, so I began to research PTSD for myself. My studies took me throughout Canada and the U.S.A., and

I began to combine and integrate the different approaches and disciplines from my extensive Massage Therapy training, Craniosacral Therapy training, SomatoEmotional Release™, and my Post Traumatic Stress training. I combined these with my personal experiences, my journaling, and self-care tools, to develop a system and approach that successfully integrated my spirit, body and mind.

For years now, I have been sharing my approach with clients and prescribing that they journal their meditations, affirmations, gratitude, intentions and connections for self-care, and from this has come the creation of Journal M.A.G.I.C.

As you read through the pages to follow, I pray that Journal M.A.G.I.C. will guide you towards capturing and realizing your magical life purpose and blessings.

Peace be with you as you embark upon this new magical chapter of your life journey.

MEDITATION

"*I* can do magical things
if I am relaxed through
breathing techniques,
meditation, visualization,
through putting attention
and intention in my body. "

Dr. Deepak Chopra
Author, Motivational
Speaker & Coach

Main Entry: MEDITATION

Definition: *(Noun) Usually refers to a state of extreme relaxation and concentration where the body is generally at rest and the mind quieted of surface thoughts.*

Synonyms: *Concentration, deep thought, introspection, pondering, reflection, rumination, self-examination, contemplation*

The conscious practice of focusing your attention intentionally on one thing at a time helps develop awareness. With greater awareness comes a better sense of presence and clarity. This helps you to understand your own mind, and the more concentrated your mind is, the deeper the calm. With regular meditation you begin to feel more focused, aware and peaceful in your life. You become more capable of making new choices in the moment and less prone to engaging in struggles, conflicts and reactions. You begin to respond rather than react, and that will ultimately lead you toward your deepest truth and a happier life. Meditation starts to bring you into balance and aligns you with a deeper part of yourself. Often, due to the 'busy-ness' of day to day life, you become disconnected, distracted and out of sorts. As you increase your meditation practice, you may find additional benefits such as: your level of relaxation deepens, attention becomes steadier, you become more self-disciplined, more adept at living in the present moment, greater stress and pain reduction, lowered blood pressure, a decrease in heart rate and numerous other physical health benefits. For these reasons, it is important to meditate every day, even if only for 5 to 15 minutes. If possible, choose to meditate at the same time and location daily.

There are various forms of meditation and the one that I feel works best with this Journal M.A.G.I.C. workbook is the 'Thank You' meditation. This mantra is very effective for shifting your consciousness and elevating your energy level. Ultimately, this will assist in your ability to receive insight into your M.A.G.I.C. inner journey meditation.

Directions: Begin by finding a place where you are free of interruption. Sit or lay down comfortably with both hands over your heart or with the palm of your left hand placed over your heart and your right hand palm over your solar plexus or belly button region. Breathe in deeply through your nose for 4 to 5 seconds and then breathe out slowly through the nose. Repeat this several times to slow down your body and mind. Be very aware of your breathing and make sure that you concentrate on every breath. Nose breathing requires focused attention on your breath and helps to slow down all that inner mind chatter. Notice your chest and ribcage rising and falling. Follow the waves of your breath and allow it to center your body and align you to the present moment. After you've become comfortable with this nose breathing technique, and you notice that you are starting to feel relaxed, begin silently repeating the words 'Thank You' on your inhalation. When you exhale, silently repeat the words 'Thank You.' Don't forget to smile. Repeat this mantra consciously, and use this deliberate nose breathing technique several times. Thank you. Thank you. Thank you.

Mindfully observe what begins to transpire within you as you continue to do this meditation daily. You will notice an elevation in your energy level, attitude, patience and overall mood. Also note how your body speaks to you in the form of physical sensations, such as a decrease in pain, tension, anxiety or stress. At this time, you can silently ask yourself a question that you want deeper insight on. This is also an excellent time for visualizing a desire, dream or intention. Have fun with this. I sometimes play and ask where a lost item is hiding and it is incredible how often I find what I am looking for as a result of meditation.

Follow your meditation with writing down your experience in your Journal M.A.G.I.C. – Meditation chapter. Recall your experience and remember how you felt while you were in your meditative state. Most of all, enjoy the process and reflect throughout the day on any new insights you have, and notice just how much more aware you have become of your thoughts and actions. Keep your Journal M.A.G.I.C. close at hand during the day, because something will strike you and you will want to capture that thought or record a change you have made as a result of your meditation. The ripples of change in your life begin with awareness of just what it is you desire to change, and that awareness comes about through meditation.

If you want to delve more deeply into Meditation, I highly recommend you study Dr. Deepak Chopra's work online.

Date:_____

Date:_____

Date: _____

Date:_____

Date:_____

Date:_____

Date: _____

Date:_____

Date:_____

Date:_____

Date:_____

Date:_____

Date:_____

Date:_____

Date: _____

MEDITATION

Date:_____

Date:_____

Date:_____

Date:_____

Date:_____

Date:_____

_____

_____

_____

_____

_____

_____

_____

_____

_____

_____

_____

_____

_____

_____

_____

_____

_____

_____

_____

_____

_____

Date:_____

Date:_____

Date:_____

_____

_____

_____

_____

_____

_____

_____

_____

_____

_____

_____

_____

_____

_____

_____

_____

_____

_____

_____

_____

_____

Date:_____

Date:_____

Date: _____

Date:_____

Date:_____

Date:_____

Date:_____

Date:_____

Date:_____

Date:_____

AFFIRMATIONS

"*Your* thoughts and beliefs of the past have created this moment and all the moments up to this moment. What you are now choosing to believe and to think and to say will create the next moment and the next day and the next month and the next year."

Louise L. Hay
Publisher, Speaker, Author, Pioneer,
Founder of Hay House Publishing

Main Entry: AFFIRMATIONS

Definition: (Noun) Declaration of the truth of something.

Synonyms: Assertion, attestation, confirmation, declaration, oath, pronouncement, statement, testament, testimonial

Our thoughts and words are creative energy. Therefore, it is vital to the process of change that you consciously direct your thoughts and words to maintain a positive outlook. Affirmations are like little reminder notes to your inner self, positive phrases that recall the change you intend to create in your life. They are always encouraging you, harnessing the power of positive thinking to keep your inner self on track.

Every word you speak and every thought you think is an affirmation. In Louise Hay's book, 'You Can Heal Your Life,' she states, *"Affirmations that are used consistently become beliefs and will always produce results, sometimes in ways we cannot even imagine."*

By taking control of your words and thoughts, you can create magic in your life. When doing your affirmations, be aware that you may experience some inner resistance. This is a definite signal that reveals any negative beliefs you may have been carrying for many years. Beliefs are not necessarily truths; they are just what you believe. This exercise of stating your affirmations out loud will provide you with an opportunity to examine the things you believe, and discern if that belief supports you and your life, or if it does not serve you. Your little reminder notes help enable you to create positive changes or eliminate unwanted negativity from your life.

In order for them to work, affirmations have to be positive and in the present tense, beginning with *"I am..."*, or *"I create...."*, or *"I have..."*, etc. State your affirmations out loud, as if you are already experiencing your desired change. Start by creating one or two of these power statements and write them down, repeating them 10 times each in this chapter. As you write them out, also read them enthusiastically out loud for best results. Read aloud your affirmations at least three times a day – morning, afternoon and evening or, better still, whenever you think of them. The best time to write your affirmations is either first thing upon waking or at night before going to bed. My personal preference is writing my affirmations before going to sleep.

There are two books I highly recommend on affirmations. The first is Louise L. Hay's 'You Can Heal Your Life', which expands upon her first book, 'Heal Your Body'. Louise Hay has made a lifetime study of mental patterns that create disease in the body, and has produced a library of authoritative work. Also available by Hay House Publishing are several 'Affirmation Card Decks', for many hours of further inspiration and personal introspection.

Her second book is entitled 'Modern Day Miracles, Louise L. Hay & Friends – Miraculous Moments and Extraordinary Stories from People All Over The World Whose Lives Have Been Touched by Louise L. Hay'. Be sure to read the first story in Chapter Two, 'A Broken Body and A Rebuilt Life.' This is my personal story of how creating my own power statements began the ripple effect that changed my life.

Date:_____

Date:_____

Date:_____

Date: _____

Date:_____

Date:_____

Date:_____

Date: _____

_____
_____
_____
_____
_____
_____
_____
_____
_____
_____
_____
_____
_____
_____
_____
_____
_____
_____
_____
_____
_____
_____
_____

Date:_____

Date:_____

Date:_____

Date: _____

AFFIRMATIONS

 69

Date:_____

Date:_____

Date:_____

Date: _____

_____

_____

_____

_____

_____

_____

_____

_____

_____

_____

_____

_____

_____

_____

_____

_____

_____

_____

_____

_____

_____

_____

Date:_____

Date: _____

Date:_____

Date:_____

Date:_____

Date:_____

Date:_____

Date:_____

Date:_____

Date:_____

Date: _____

Date:_____

Date:_____

Date: _____

Date:_____

Date: _____

AFFIRMATIONS

GRATITUDE

"*Being* in a state of gratitude actually creates magnetism and of course, a magnet draws things to itself. By giving authentic thanks for all the good you now have as well as the challenges, through this magnetism you'll start the flow of more good into your life."

Dr. Wayne Dyer
Author, Motivational Speaker

Main Entry: *GRATITUDE*

Definition: *(Noun) The quality or feeling of being grateful or thankful.*

Synonyms: *Appreciation, acknowledgement, grace, thankfulness, honor, praise, recognition, gratefulness, thanks, thanksgiving*

A Gratitude Journal consciously calls attention to the things we are thankful for each day: what we have received, what we gave, or what we've contributed to. By focusing on gratitude, we become aware of these things and thus shift our thinking to the positive.

Developing an attitude of gratitude toward the people, things and events in your life is a life-affirming and effective way to strengthen your emotional resilience, while reducing stress, ridding your mind of dis-ease, and easing conflicts. Maintaining a gratitude journal makes it easy to get into the habit of focusing on the positive in your life, while also enjoying the benefits of journaling.

Cultivating an attitude of gratitude and recording it in your journal reaps numerous benefits. Research suggests that people who are particularly grateful have higher levels of well being. Grateful people are happier, less depressed and more satisfied with their lives and relationships. They have higher levels of control over their environment, personal growth, purpose in life and self acceptance. Research also indicates that people who practice gratitude on a daily basis are healthier and are more effective in the world.

Gratitude journals are useful tools for stress management. Journaling also increases the positive energy flow and creates an environment conducive to bringing about remarkable changes in your life, in miraculous ways.

Begin your Gratitude journal by listing 10 people, places or things that you are grateful for. You can make a list or compose a more descriptive paragraph on each item. It is important to make sure that you are sincerely feeling grateful, an intense emotion that must be present for the best results. Be sure to write Thank you, Thank you, Thank you, after each gratitude. The optimal time to write in your Gratitude journal is either first thing in the morning or at night before you go to bed. It's important to be in a quiet and calm place, free of interruptions, when you are doing your reflecting and writing.

Review your day and consider each area of your life: relationships, health, career, finances, spiritual growth, contribution and fun. Include anything that was a source of gratitude for you today. With consistent practice and persistence, you will begin to see situations change almost magically. As you focus on the blessings in your life, you will begin to attract more positive energy and magnetize things towards you.

Therein lies the magic of expressing gratitude in your journal every day. Like the drop of water whose concentric rings ripple outward, it connects you to a state of appreciation that extends into everything you do, say and experience. It inspires you to view your life from a state of grace. I highly recommend you view a YouTube video called 'Gratitude' by Dr. Wayne Dyer, and check out his other works online.

Date:_____

Date:_____

GRATITUDE

Date:_____

Date:_____

Date:_____

Date:_____

Date:_____

Date:_____

Date:_____

Date:_____

GRATITUDE

Date:_____

Date: _____

Date:_____

Date: _____

Date:_____

Date:_____

Date:_____

GRATITUDE

Date:_____

Date: _____

Date:_____

Date:_____

Date:_____

Date:_____

Date: _____

GRATITUDE

Date:_____

Date:_____

Date:_____

Date: _____

Date: _____

GRATITUDE

INTENTIONS

"*W*hen we marry intention
with action, miracles happen."

Cheryl Richardson
Author, Motivational
Speaker & Coach

Main Entry:	INTENTIONS

Definition:	*(Noun) A course of action that one intends to follow. An aim that guides action; an objective; to have in mind a purpose or plan; to direct the mind to aim.*

Synonyms:	*Aim, ambition, aspiration, dream, goal, idea, ideal, objective, target*

The Intentions Journal is designed to keep you moving forward and is a powerful way to create magic in your life. Setting specific intentions keeps you focused on what's important to you and keeps you on the track of creating your deepest desires and dreams.

Writing out your intentions in your Journal M.A.G.I.C. workbook activates the left brain and grounds your purpose in conscious physical reality. When you set intentions and then act on them, it sets in motion a whole thinking process that demonstrates your commitment. It creates an ideal setting for magical things to occur.

Lacking goals or a sense of purpose can cause us to meander through life with neither meaning nor direction. With a clearly defined and precise intention, all the forces of the Universe align to make possible even the most impossible.

You can set intentions for your day, week, month or year, or for several years ahead. Be as specific as possible. For example, *"Today,* (include the date), *I intend to… ; Tomorrow, I intend to … and have a completed date by* (Insert the date). *"* Consider what you most desire to happen in your life. Begin with brainstorming your ideas, goals and deepest desires. It is important to imagine that money is no barrier; that it is not even a factor in your life. Now, take 5 minutes to write down everything that you desire; everything that comes to your mind. The next step is to narrow it down and select the top 3 intentions from your list.

If you are having difficulty identifying or setting out your intentions, these questions may give you a little insight and assistance: *"What do I want to achieve?"*, *"Why do I want to achieve this,"* and *"How can I achieve this?"*

Look at the various facets of your life, such as relationships, health, career, finances, spiritual growth, contribution and fun. It is always important to include a target date for completing or reaching your dreams, goals and intentions, even making simple yet powerful intentions — for example, *"Today I intend to smile at everyone I see"*; or *"Today I intend to look into the eyes of each person I meet"*. Observe the impact this has on the lives of others, as well as on yourself. Defining and setting out your intentions is similar to using a GPS for your vehicle. You have to know where you currently are and where you'd like to go for the GPS to do its magic and help you to reach your destination effectively and efficiently.

Another fun way to help set your intentions is with decks of cards. There are numerous wonderful card decks by various authors to choose from — I have several at my office and use them — and can personally recommend 'Self Care' and 'Grace Cards' by Cheryl Richardson.

Creating intentions is the single most important investment you can make in yourself. Let's face it, you are the most valuable and precious asset you possess! Your intentions will be like that drop of water, sending positive energy rippling throughout your life in all directions.

INTENTIONS

Date: _____

Date:_____

Date:_____

Date:_____

Date:_____

INTENTIONS

Date:_____

Date:_____

INTENTIONS

Date:_____

Date:_____

Date:_____

INTENTIONS

Date:_____

Date:_____

INTENTIONS

Date:_____

Date: _____

INTENTIONS

Date:_____

Date: _____

Date:_____

Date:_____

Date:_____

Date:_____

Date:_____

Date:

INTENTIONS

Date:_____

Date: _____

Date:_____

Date:_____

INTENTIONS

Date:_____

Date:_____

Date:_____

Date:_____

INTENTIONS

171

Date:_____

INTENTIONS

"*When* you write down your thoughts, feelings, and concerns, you begin to make connections that you never saw before. Keeping such a record and watching how you're growing is a powerful tool for helping you make connections between feelings, symptoms, beliefs, emotions and choices on a daily basis."

Christiane Northrup, M.D., Author

CONNECTIONS

Main Entry: CONNECTIONS

Definition: *(Noun) Something that communicates, relates, connects; that is linked with another; associated with; that there is a relationship between two or more things.*

Synonyms: *Affinity, association, bearing, bond, correlation, interrelation, link, nexus, liaison, partnership, relation, relevance, tie-in, togetherness*

The Connections Journal is where we connect all the pieces. We continually receive messages in many forms throughout the day; most of the time you are not even consciously aware of them. These messages show up right in front of you, in many ways and forms. You'll see a message on a passing vehicle, a bumper sticker, a license plate, a billboard; you will read a quote, hear lyrics in a song, or experience any number of things that resonate within you. Whatever the inspiration, it will actually relate to what you are thinking about, experiencing, contemplating or possibly even re-affirming as your path. You can also receive messages or make connections while in your 'dream state.' In addition to recording the random inspirations you receive as you navigate your day, you'll be able to track any of your dreams in this chapter. Here is where you can journal your thoughts and feelings anytime throughout the day. Use your Journal M.A.G.I.C. workbook to record your special moments, deeper insights or clarity, and the ripple of connections begins.

When you begin to consciously open up, you will start noticing deeper meanings, clues, patterns, and symbols. These will come to you in vivid dreams, or visions that appear in your head while meditating, or you will open up to your intuition and listen more closely to that inner voice in your head and heart.

Whenever the 'light bulb' comes on and you have an 'aha' moment or a brainstorm of ideas, this is the section where you record it. You may not always be conscious of all the connections, but by tracking them on a daily basis and writing them down, you will make more connections than you have ever made, and become aware of messages you haven't seen before.

Connections may occur from reviewing one of the previous chapters in your Journal M.A.G.I.C. workbook entries. Keeping track of these inspirations will lead you to greater awareness, expanded consciousness and greater creativity. It assists you in discovering the meanings in the multitude of messages that you receive daily, and helps you be more conscious of the messages that guide and direct you throughout each day. Connections (sometimes recognized as synchronicities) are a way to help you focus, pay attention, and be present in the moment.

Through keeping your 'connections' written record, you will begin to see how you're growing, evolving and making changes to your life. You will start to realize just how things seem to be magically coming together, and yes, how everything is connected. Connection is a very powerful tool, as our minds open up to a world of new possibilities.

These unexpected gifts of guidance drop into our minds and ripple concentrically out into the Universe to influence us and others. Connections dictate the direction of our lives and the choices we make; they help to determine the people we touch. Connections impact each and every one of us every day, and affect our personal world in infinite ways.

Dr. Christiane Northrup, M.D. and Author stated, *"When we find the connection between our thoughts, beliefs, physical health and life circumstances, we find that we are in the driver's seat of our lives and can make profound changes. Nothing is more exhilarating or empowering."*

Visit http://www.drnorthrup.com for healing wisdom and daily inspirations.

Date:_____

Date:_____

CONNECTIONS

Date: _____

Date:_____

Date: _____

Date:_____

Date:_____

CONNECTIONS

Date:_____

Date: _____

Date:_____

Date: _____

CONNECTIONS

Date:_____

Date: _____

Date:_____

CONNECTIONS

Date: _____

Date:_____

Date:_____

Date:_____

Date:_____

CONNECTIONS

Date:_____

Date:_____

CONNECTIONS

Date:_____

Date:_____

Date:_____

Date:_____

CONNECTIONS

Date:_____

CONNECTIONS

Date:_____

Date:_____

"We all have intuitive gifts, the magic comes in realizing how to trust their natural guidance."

Caroline Myss,
Author, Medical Intuitive

Acknowledgements

I have been blessed with so many wonderful teachers in my life. To every person who has crossed my path, whether for a moment, a month or a lifetime, I am indebted to you for all the experiences and lessons I've learned. I have been touched in ways you may never know, for you have contributed to the growth of who I am, the things I do and say, and the legacy that I will leave to my children.

I would like to thank my family, specifically my late parents, Lina and Claude: my greatest teachers, whose unwavering love, faith and support have shaped me to become the person that I am. I am forever grateful. You are eternally in my heart, soul and prayers.

To my precious and wonderful children, Alexa and Cameron: you are my greatest gifts, teachers and inspiration. I love you both to infinity and beyond. I am very proud of the incredible treasures you are; I am truly blessed to be on this journey of life with you.

To the many wonderful teachers I have had the honor of working with: it is a privilege to learn from you. Some of you came in the form of books, feeding my passion for learning and endless possibilities. Some of my favorite authors and quotes I share in this journal.

To my courageous and brave clients: I am humbled by your spirit and commitment to growth and healing. I am always in awe of the capacity of the human spirit and its ability to overcome life's challenges through faith, appreciation, confidence, trust and love.

A special thanks to my dear friends whose love, loyalty and support is unconditional. You know who you are and I truly cherish our life journey together!

Heartfelt thanks to Beth McBlain, my editor who believed in the importance of this Journal M.A.G.I.C. workbook from the beginning. Your passion, enthusiasm and attention to detail are all truly inspiring. I thank you for helping to make this book a reality.

I am especially grateful to my ultimate love source: God. You are the light within me that inspires me to always do my best, and feeds the fire inside me to assist people along their healing and life journey.

About the Author

Hair and photo by Daniel Fiorio, Toronto

Martez Schembri is a Registered Massage Therapist, Craniosacral Therapist, SomatoEmotional Release™, Educator, Compassion Fatigue Specialist, Lecturer and Author.

She is the owner of *Hands On Health Care*, established in 1993 in Whitby, Canada. She has continued to develop her very own personal style of balancing *Spirit, Body and Mind* through **Integrative Craniosacral Therapy** that evolved as a result of her own healing journey from a head-on automobile collision 25 years ago.

Martez provides a unique approach to balancing the spirit, body, mind and emotions for trauma, stress, pain management and self care. She believes in an integrative holistic approach to healthcare in the areas of Emotional Release, Shock, Trauma, Post Traumatic Stress Disorder, Compassion Fatigue and Body-Oriented Stress Management.

Martez's passion is to empower, educate and inspire people to heal themselves on all levels. That is how Journal M.A.G.I.C. evolved into a workbook for others to track their journey.

She enjoys educating and sharing her skills and her Journal M.A.G.I.C. workbook with anyone interested in her experience and knowledge. Martez has taught at Durham College, Centennial College's Massage Therapy Program and has lectured in the United States and Canada. She has been interviewed on national television and international radio. Her story has also been documented and published in Louise Hay's *Modern Day Miracles.*

To learn more about Martez, check out her website http://www.handsonhealthcare.org or call her directly at (905) 242-1110.

Martez Schembri

A noted educator, lecturer and author, Martez is the proprietor of *Hands On Health Care* in Whitby, Canada (established in 1993). Over the years, Martez has developed her unique style of balancing spirit, body, and mind through Integrative Craniosacral Therapy and other modalities, including Shock &Trauma Release Therapy.